Christmas Greetings

I0866989

Create a Christmas treasure to display in your home or to offer special wishes to someone you hold dear. Golden charms add elegance to these three designs, which were adapted from vintage greeting cards.

LEISURE ARTS, INC. • Maumelle, Arkansas

A
MERRY
CHRISTMAS
TO YOU

The merry chimes of Christmastime bring joy and peace to you
May Christmas joys be thine

Santa Claus Book

X	DMC	1/4X	1/2X	B'ST
•	blanc		8	*
\	312			
⊕	321			
P	322		+	
◎	334			
H	352			
⁘	353			
	356			/
▶	433			
5	434			
U	436			
=	437			
•	469			
4	470			
Π	471			
•	498			
	640		✔	
☆	642		*	
Λ	644		Σ	
◊	666			
♡	676			
%	677			
+	680			
◒	729			ø
×	758			
⊥	822		♥	
✔	902			
T	937			
◊	948			
O	3031			/
⁘	3064			
()	3708			
△	3755			
V	3801			

Green area indicates last row of previous section of design.

* Work in long stitches.

STITCH COUNT (124w x 78h)

14 count	8 7/8"	x	5 5/8"
16 count	7 3/4"	x	4 7/8"
18 count	7"	x	4 3/8"

Santa Claus Book (shown on page 2): The design was stitched over 2 fabric threads on a 17" x 14" piece of Cream Cashel Linen® (28 ct). Two strands of floss were used for Cross Stitch and 1 strand for Half Cross Stitch and Backstitch. To complete book, see Finishing Instructions, page 12.

Needlework adaptation by Carol Emmer.

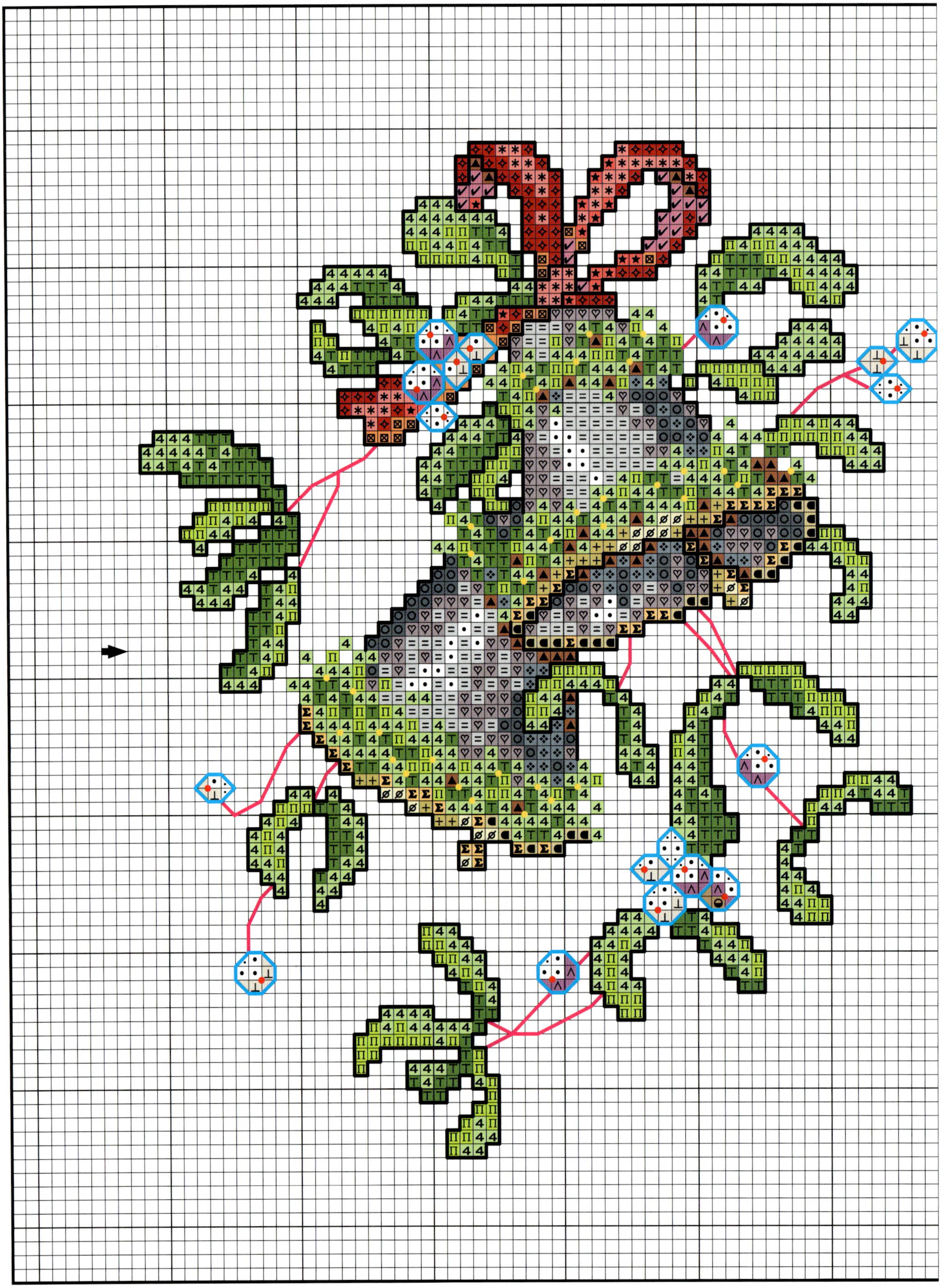

X	DMC	¼X	B'ST	X	DMC	¼X	X	DMC	¼X	B'ST
•	blanc	◩		○	647		T	937	◩	
★	321	◩		=	648		▲	3031		/
P	469		/*	✧	666		♡	3072		
4	470	◩		+	676		*	3801	◩	
Π	471			ø	677		●	646	French Knot	
⊠	498	◩		◖	680		●	Mill Hill Bead - 42013		
◒	642	◩		Σ	729					
∧	644	◩		⊥	822	◩				
❖	646		/	✔	902					

Green area indicates last row of previous section of design.

* Work in long stitches.

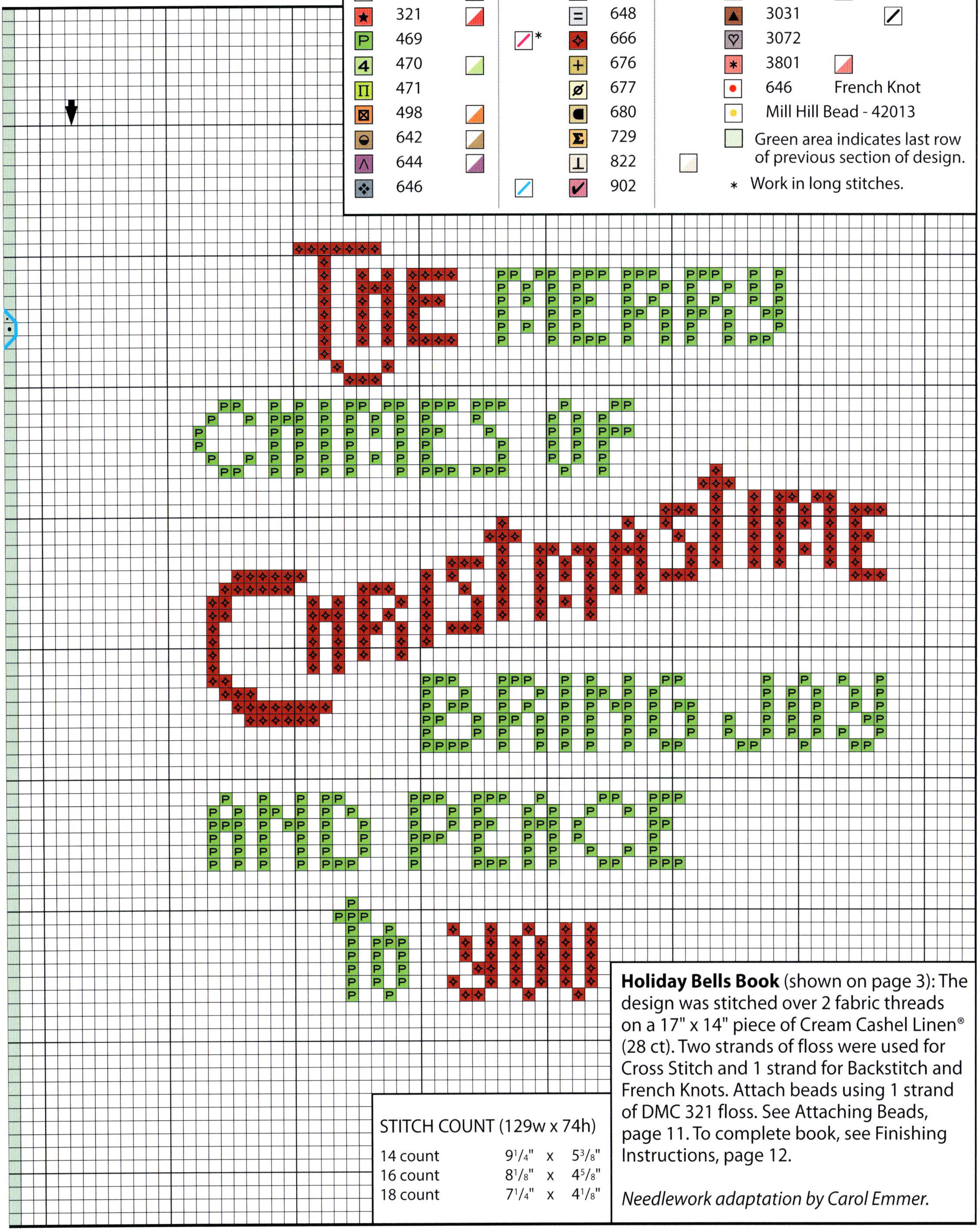

STITCH COUNT (129w x 74h)

14 count	9¼"	x	5⅜"
16 count	8⅛"	x	4⅝"
18 count	7¼"	x	4⅛"

Holiday Bells Book (shown on page 3): The design was stitched over 2 fabric threads on a 17" x 14" piece of Cream Cashel Linen® (28 ct). Two strands of floss were used for Cross Stitch and 1 strand for Backstitch and French Knots. Attach beads using 1 strand of DMC 321 floss. See Attaching Beads, page 11. To complete book, see Finishing Instructions, page 12.

Needlework adaptation by Carol Emmer.

X	DMC	B'ST
☆	321	
II	469	
8	470	
C	471	
⊠	498	/
◇	666	
*	676	
♥	902	
ø	937	
	3031	/
T	3801	

Green area indicates last row of previous section of design.

STITCH COUNT (132w x 81h)

14 count	9 1/2"	x	5 7/8"
16 count	8 1/4"	x	5 1/8"
18 count	7 3/8"	x	4 1/2"

Christmas Joys Book (shown on page 3): The design was stitched over 2 fabric threads on a 17" x 14" piece of Cream Cashel Linen® (28 ct). Two strands of floss were used for Cross Stitch and 1 strand for Backstitch. To complete book, see Finishing Instructions, page 12.

Needlework adaptation by Carol Emmer.

General Instructions

HOW TO READ CHARTS

Each chart is made up of a key and a gridded design on which each square represents a stitch. The symbols in the key tell which floss color to use for each stitch in the chart. The following headings and symbols are given:

X — Cross Stitch
DMC — DMC color number
¹/₄X — Quarter Stitch
¹/₂X — Half Cross Stitch
B'ST — Backstitch
COLOR — The name given to the floss color in this chart

A square filled with a color and a symbol should be worked as a Cross Stitch.

A triangle should be worked as a Quarter Stitch.

A square containing a colored symbol should be worked as a Half Cross Stitch.

A straight line should be worked as a Backstitch.

A large dot listed near the end of the key should be worked as a French Knot or it may indicate bead placement.

Sometimes the symbol for a Cross Stitch may be partially covered when a Backstitch crosses the square. Refer to the background color to determine the floss color.

HOW TO STITCH

Always work Cross Stitches, Quarter Stitches, and Half Cross Stitches first and then add the Backstitch and French Knots.

Preparing Fabric

To prevent raveling, overcast raw edges of the fabric.

Working with Floss

To ensure smoother stitches, separate strands and realign them before threading the needle. Keep stitching tension consistent. Begin and end floss by running under several stitches on the back; never tie knots.

Where to Start

The horizontal and vertical centers of each charted design are shown by arrows. You may start at any point on the charted design, but be sure the design will be centered on the fabric. Locate the center of the fabric by folding it in half, top to bottom and again left to right. On the charted design, count the number of squares (stitches) from the center of the chart to where you wish to start. Then, from the fabric's center, find your starting point by counting out twice the number of fabric threads (stitches).

To add support to stitches, it is important that the first Cross Stitch is placed on the fabric with stitch 1-2 beginning and ending where a vertical fabric thread crosses over a horizontal fabric thread (*Fig. 1*). When the first stitch is in the correct position, the entire design will be placed properly, with vertical fabric threads supporting each stitch.

Fig. 1

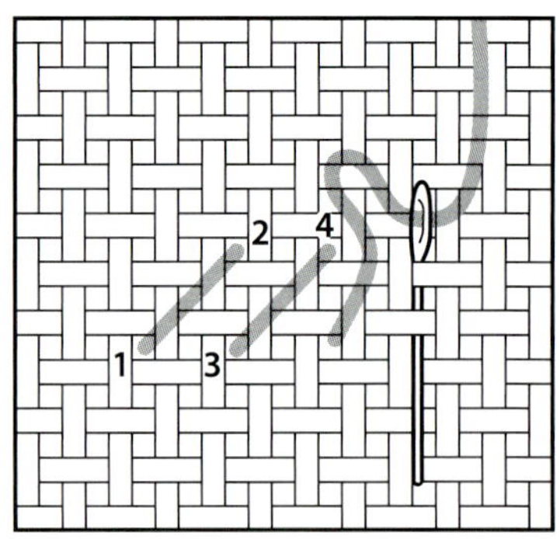

STITCH DIAGRAMS

When stitching, bring the threaded needle up at 1 and all odd numbers and down at 2 and all even numbers.

Cross Stitch (X): For horizontal rows, work stitches in two journeys *(Fig. 2)*. For vertical rows, complete each stitch as shown *(Fig. 3)*.

Fig. 2

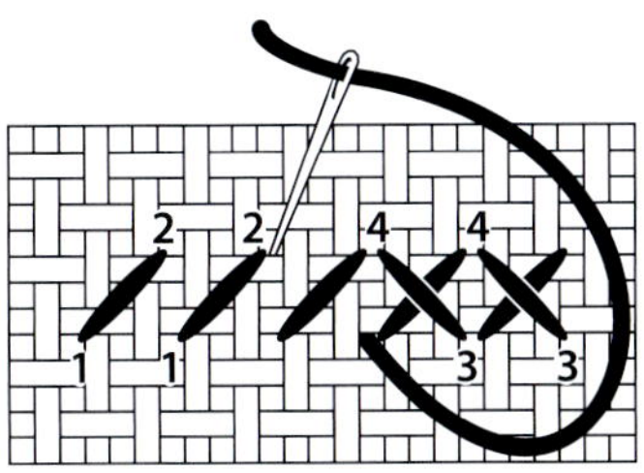

Fig. 3

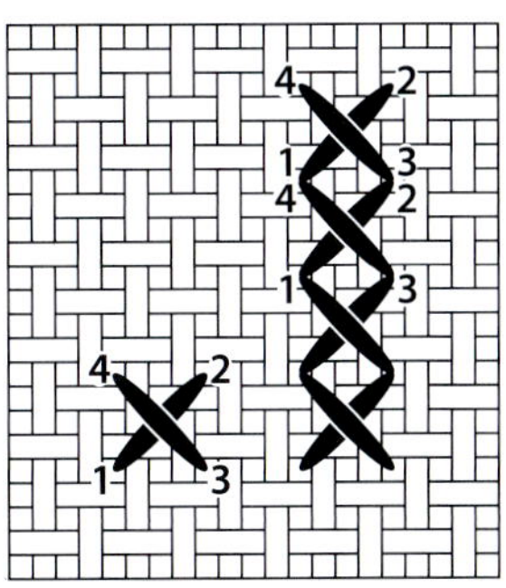

Quarter Stitch (1/4X): Come up at 1 *(Fig. 4)*, and then go down at 2.

Fig. 4

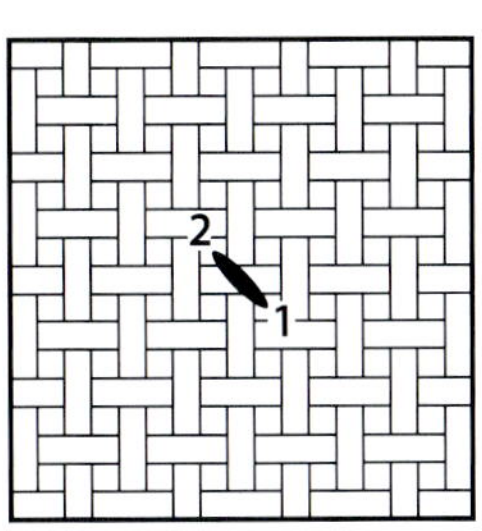

Half Cross Stitch (1/2X): This stitch is one journey of the Cross Stitch and is worked from the lower left to the upper right as shown in *Fig. 5*.

Fig. 5

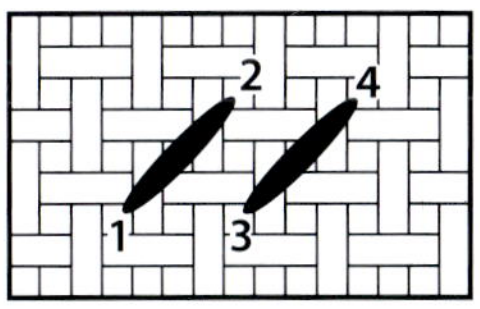

Backstitch (B'ST): For outlines and details, Backstitch should be worked after the design has been completed *(Fig. 6)*.

Fig. 6

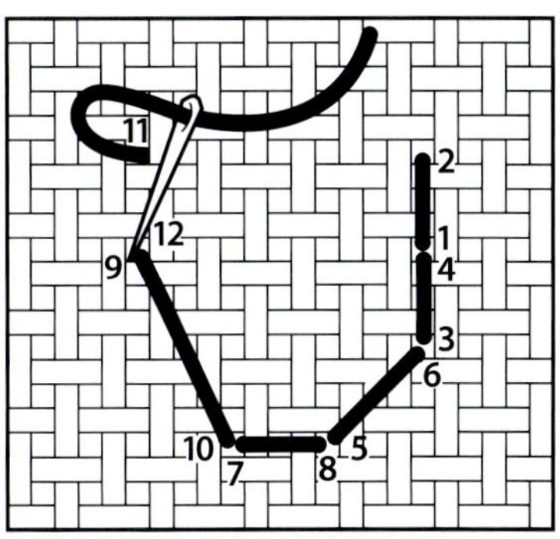

French Knot: Bring the needle up at 1. Wrap the floss once around the needle. Insert the needle at 2, tighten the knot, and pull the needle through the fabric, holding the floss until it must be released *(Fig. 7)*. For a larger knot, use more floss strands and wrap only once.

Fig. 7

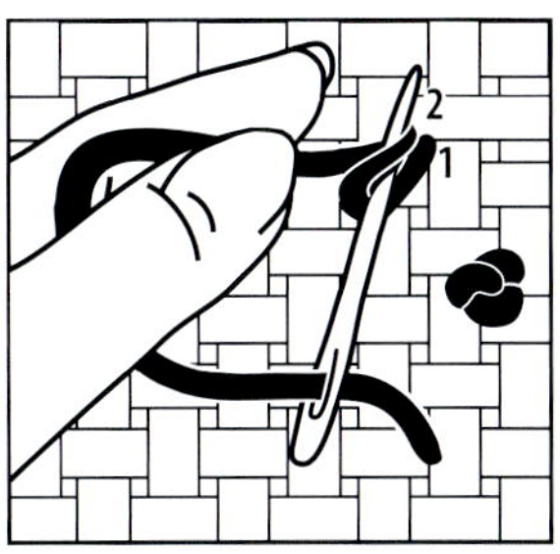

ADDITIONAL TECHNIQUES

Attaching Beads

Use one strand of floss that matches the bead and a fine needle that will pass through the bead. Secure floss on the back of the fabric. Bring the needle up where indicated on the chart, then run the needle through the bead and down through the fabric *(Fig. 8)*. To make the bead stand upright, run needle back through bead, making an "X". Secure the floss on the back or move to the next bead.

Fig. 8

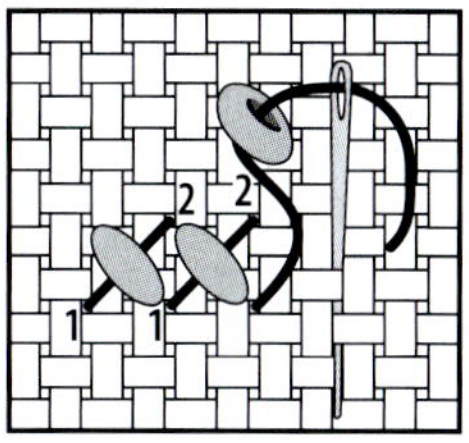

The Sewing Method

Cross Stitches should be worked over two fabric threads on linen fabric. When working over two fabric threads, you may choose to use the sewing method instead of the stab method.

To use the sewing method, keep your stitching hand on the right side of the fabric (instead of stabbing the fabric with the needle and taking your stitching hand to the back of the fabric to pick up the needle). With the sewing method, you take the needle down and up with one stroke instead of two.

Finishing Instructions

For each book, you will need an 11" x 8" piece of fabric for backing, four $4^3/_4$" x $6^3/_4$" pieces of adhesive mounting board, four $4^3/_4$" x $6^3/_4$" pieces of batting, 36" length of $^1/_4$" diameter purchased cording with attached seam allowance, $10^1/_2$" length of $^3/_8$" wide ribbon, clear-drying craft glue, and assorted charms.

After stitching design, refer to photo for placement and attach charms to stitched piece using 1 strand of floss that matches fabric.

Centering design, trim stitched piece to 11" x 8".

Remove paper from one mounting board piece and press one batting piece onto mounting board. Repeat with remaining mounting board and batting pieces. To make curved outer edges, trim corners on one long edge of each board/batting.

With the curved corners of one board to the ***left***, center wrong side of left half of stitched piece over batting. With the curved corners of a second board to the ***right*** and allowing a $^1/_2$" space between the boards, center wrong side of right half of stitched piece over batting ***(Fig. 9)***.

Fig. 9

Fold edges of stitched piece to back of boards and glue in place.

For book back, repeat with backing fabric and remaining boards.

Beginning and ending at bottom center of stitched piece, glue cording seam allowance to wrong side of book front, overlapping ends of cording. Glue one end of ribbon to wrong side of book front at center top.

Holding ribbon out of the way, match wrong sides and align boards; glue book front and back together. Allow to dry completely. Machine stitch book through all layers at center space between boards. Trim ribbon as desired.

Production Team: Technical Writer – Frances Huddleston; Technical Associates – Mary Hutcheson and Lisa Lancaster; Editorial Writer – Susan Frantz Wiles; Senior Graphic Artist – Lora Puls; Graphic Artist – Victoria Temple; Photostylist – Sondra Daniel; Photographer – Ken West.